© Brown Wells and Jacobs Limited London 1990
Written by Brian Jones
Illustrated by Julian Baum

This 1990 edition published by
Crescent Books
Distributed by Crown Publishers, Inc
225 Park Avenue South,
New York, New York 10003

Printed and bound in Belgium

ISBN 0-517-01991-4

8 7 6 5 4 3 2 1

THE ASTRONOMER'S
NIGHT SKY

A beginner's guide to the
Sun, Stars and Planets

Text by Brian Jones
Illustrated by Julian Baum

CRESCENT BOOKS
New York

INTRODUCTION

Astronomy is the science of the cosmos. But it differs from other sciences in that those who study it are unable to touch and feel what they see. Astronomers can only watch the Sun, Moon, planets and stars from afar.

The Universe is very beautiful, and it can be studied by anyone who cares to look up at the sky. You don't need a telescope, or even a pair of binoculars, to get to know the night sky. Just looking at it, and reading a guide to help you to understand what you are seeing, will help you to become familiar with its stars and planets.

The Astonomer's Night Sky is such a guide. Within its pages you will find introductions to the Sun and the planets which share our region of space. Eclipses, comets, meteors and meteorites are included, and the book also looks to the Universe beyond the Solar System where there are boundless numbers of stars, some smaller than the Sun, some larger; huge clouds of interstellar dust and gas; clusters of stars; stars

which vary in brightness, and stars which belong to binary and multiple star systems. Our own Galaxy contains countless numbers of each type of object. There are also many other galaxies scattered throughout the Universe, some on their own in space and some which are members of huge collections or clusters of galaxies, whose vastness defies the imagination. The book also looks at the future of man's exploration of space, and where our inquisitive nature might take us as we attempt to discover the secrets of the Universe in which we live.

A series of star charts shows the main groups of stars visible during each of the four seasons, from the northern hemisphere, looking north and south. Highlights of each season are given, together with details of objects which can be seen with the unaided eye, with binoculars, and with a small telescope. The charts provide a permanent and readily accessible reference as you set off on your exploration of the Universe.

Happy stargazing!

THE SUN

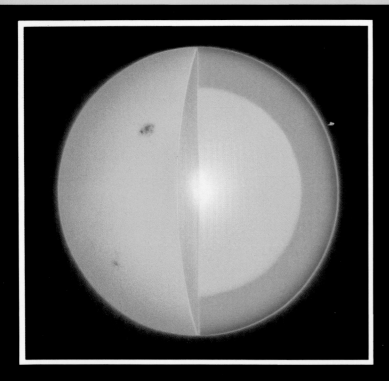

A cross-section of the Sun showing the hot, central core (white) where the Sun's energy is created. This energy is carried outwards through different zones of the Sun's interior to the surface from where it escapes as light and heat.

THE SUN

Although the Sun appears to be the brightest star in the sky, this is only because it is so close to us compared with the other stars in our galaxy. Its diameter is a colossal 865,000 miles and its light and heat makes life on our planet possible. Because the Sun is so close to us, astronomers are able to study it quite easily. Its surface activity is continually monitored, giving useful information about the Sun and similar stars.

All our observations of the Sun are made from over its equator. This is because the Earth (and all the other planets) travels around the Sun over its equatorial regions. But a spacecraft called Ulysees, which is to be launched in late 1990, will fly over the Sun's north and south poles and observe it from there.

HOW THE SUN SHINES

The huge amounts of energy that pour from the Sun are created at its core. The temperature here is a staggering 27,000,000 degrees Fahrenheit, and the pressure is equal to a third of a million times that at the Earth's surface. Under these extreme conditions, the Sun's hydrogen is crushed to form the heavier gas helium. During this reaction, a tiny amount of hydrogen slowly makes its way to the Sun's surface from which it escapes as light and heat. The total amount of hydrogen lost by the Sun is equal to four million tons every second! Yet there is no cause to worry. The Sun has been shining this way for 5,000 million years and such are its reserves of hydrogen it will continue to do so for a further 5,000 million years.

SOLAR ACTIVITY

Sunspots are the most prominent feature to be seen on the Sun's surface. They look like dark spots because their temperature is a mere 7,200 degrees Fahrenheit compared with that of the photosphere (the visible surface of the Sun) which is 10,800 degrees Fahrenheit, and they therefore shine less brightly.

Although some sunspots are quite tiny and barely visible, some can be many thousands of miles across. Some have even been large enough to be visible to the naked eye! (WARNING: To observe the Sun safely special methods are used – see end of text.)

Except for the smallest ones, sunspots have a dark central region (the umbra) surrounded by a lighter area (the penumbra). They last, on average, for around two months. Sunspot activity increases and decreases over a regular eleven-year cycle, which was first pointed out in 1843 by the German astronomer Heinrich Schwabe. By timing how long it takes for a sunspot to travel across the visible disc of the Sun, astronomers have been able to work out the Sun's rotation period. This is equal to roughly 25 days at the equator, and 35 days at the poles. This is made possible because the Sun is not a solid body, but is composed of hot gases.

Other features which may be observed on the Sun's surface include faculae and prominences. Faculae are luminous clouds of gas, mainly hydrogen, which are seen above areas where sunspots are about to form. Prominences are huge columns of gas which appear above sunspots. There are two types: eruptive

Here we see a telescope being used to focus an image of the Sun onto a screen. Many new telescopes are supplied with solar screens and special clamps to hold them in place on the telescope body. This is the only safe way to observe the Sun, and good images of the solar disc may be obtained.

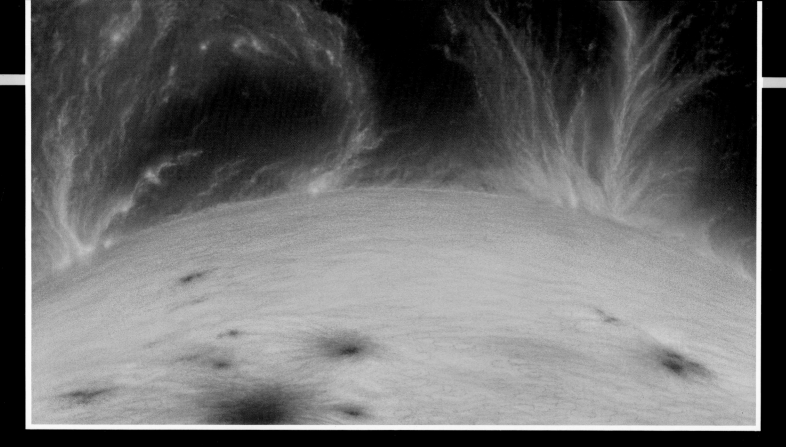

prominences, formed from gas leaving the Sun at speeds up to 600 miles or more a second, which can change shape very quickly, and quiescent prominences, which are more stable and sometimes hang suspended over the Sun's surface for several days.

The most lively of all solar activities are flares which, are bright streamers of hot gas. Their temperatures can shoot up to several millions of degrees in a very short time. Flares contribute greatly to the number of energised particles coming from the Sun and large flares can produce intense displays of aurorae in the Earth's atmosphere. Aurorae occur when energised particles from the Sun collide with air particles, making them shine and producing the eerie glow often referred to as the Northern (or Southern) Lights.

THE SOLAR WIND

Energy coming from the Sun leaves its surface, or photosphere, and passes through a much cooler region, the chromosphere. This is where faculae and flares are seen. It then passes through the outer region of the Sun's atmosphere, the corona, which stretches for several million miles above the solar surface. It is in the corona that prominences occur.

The constant stream of energised particles leaving the Sun is called the solar wind. It travels almost 9,000 miles, before giving way to interstellar space. Where this happens is considered to be the true outer limit of the solar system.

OBSERVING THE SUN

NEVER look at the Sun through a telescope, or any other form of optical aid! Instead, use the telescope to project an image of the Sun on to a screen such as a piece of white card, rather like the way you use a magnifying glass to focus the Sun's light and heat to a point. Also, NEVER look through the telescope or

In this view looking across the Sun's photosphere we see huge prominences leaping up above the solar surface. In the foreground are several groups of sunspots, these somewhat cooler regions appearing as dark patches on the brighter yellow photosphere.

viewfinder whilst doing this. Even a glimpse of the concentrated image of the Sun formed by the telescope could blind you. It may take longer to pick up the Sun's image with the telescope in this way, but it is a much safer way of studying the Sun.

A ring of auroral activity is seen here around the Earth's northern magnetic pole. Although aurorae are not uncommon, vivid displays can take place when the Sun is particularly active. At these times, the number of energised particles bombarding the Earth's atmosphere can rise substantially, producing an increase in the size and number of auroral displays.

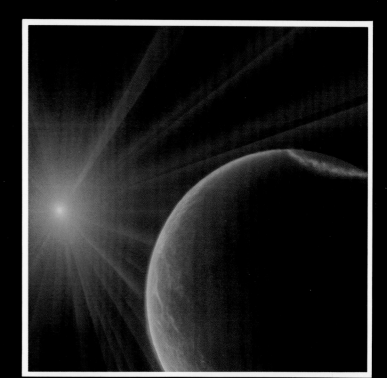

MERCURY

Mercury is the closest planet to the Sun, which makes its position comparatively easy to find. It is usually seen low over the horizon, either in the east before sunrise, or in the west after sunset. Thus it is never seen against a truly dark sky, and because of this astronomers have always found it difficult to observe its surface details. Mercury orbits the Sun once every 88 days.

We didn't get a good look at Mercury until the American Mariner 10 craft flew past the planet three times in 1974 and 1975. Its cameras revealed craters, mountains, ridges and valleys.

Once a planet of mystery, Mercury was seen to be a barren, desolate and uninviting world. The most

A view across the hot, barren Mercurian surface. The Sun, only around 36 million miles away, appears much larger than it does from Earth. Features typical of the surface of the innermost planet, such as mountains and crater walls, can be seen here.

common feature Mariner 10 recorded were craters, which pepper most of the planet's surface. In many ways Mercury resembles the Moon, although it has fewer dark plains than can be seen on the Moon's surface.

It also has a number of long, meandering cliffs called scarps, some of which tower almost two miles above the surrounding terrain. One of the largest features recorded was the Caloris Basin, a huge bowl 800 miles in diameter, which was created by the impact of a large meteoroid some 3.5 billion years ago. The Caloris Basin is surrounded by mountains over a mile high.

Mercury has an extremely thin atmosphere, made up mainly of vaporized sodium. Mercury's atmosphere is so thin that it is better than any vacuum that can be produced in a laboratory on Earth. Because the atmosphere is so thin, the temperature drops alarmingly at night. In the daytime, it can reach 797 degrees Fahrenheit on the equator at noon. However, because there is no atmosphere to retain the heat (unlike the Earth), this can plummet to a frigid −300 degrees Farenheit just before sunrise.

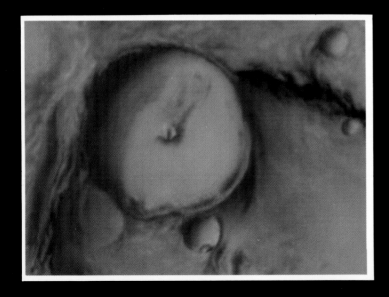

This view shows the crater Kuiper, the first crater to be indentified during the approach to Mercury of Mariner 10 in March 1974. Kuiper has a diameter of around 40 miles and intrudes into the larger, 80 mile diameter crater Murasaki, part of which can be seen here.

VENUS

Venus is the second planet out from the Sun and the closest planet to the Earth. It orbits the Sun once every 225 days. The length of a "day" on Venus (the time it takes to spin once on its axis) is 243 Earth-days, which means that the Venusian day is longer than its year!

Like Mercury, Venus is seen either in the east before sunrise or in the west after sunset. But because it is further away from the Sun, it can often be seen against a dark sky. It is the brightest object in the sky, apart from the Sun and Moon. This is because Venus is covered in dense white clouds which reflect sunlight extremely well, but which permanently hide the surface from view.

The atmosphere reaches to a height of about 150 miles, although it is densest near the surface. The surface pressure on Venus is 90 times that at the Earth's surface!

As well as creating this phenomenal pressure, the atmosphere also holds back much of the heat from the Sun which filters through to the planet's surface, just like the glass in a greenhouse which lets the Sun's heat in, then tends to keep it there. That's why it is always warmer inside a greenhouse than outside. This so-called "greenhouse effect", means that the surface temperature on Venus can reach a staggering 842 degrees Fahrenheit!

To make things even more unpleasant, the Venusian clouds contain droplets of sulphuric acid. This means that if you ventured onto the planet's surface without protective clothing, you would be crushed, fried and baked very quickly! Venus is certainly an unwelcoming place, and it is no wonder that space probes which have landed on the planet have only remained operational for a short time.

In spite of the dense clouds covering the planet, however, special instruments carried on these probes have allowed us to map the surface. These instruments send down radar pulses which "bounce off" the surface

and back to the spacecraft. Scientists can tell how high the ground is under the craft by timing how long it takes for the signals to come back, just like a battleship can tell how far away an enemy ship is by timing how long it takes radar beams to bounce back from it. If the radar beam from a space probe hits a mountain it will have less distance to travel. This means that it will return to the spacecraft faster than if it had hit a flat plain or a valley floor.

Many of the different materials given out by Earth's volcanoes have been found in the Venusian atmosphere, and it seems that this material is constantly being replaced by active volcanoes on the planet. Maxwell Montes, the largest mountain on Venus, is thought by many astronomers to be a huge volcano. Orbiting spacecraft have also detected what appear to be lightning bolts similar to those which occur above erupting volcanoes here on Earth.

Venus (upper left) and Mercury are seen here in the twilight sky.

EARTH

Because the Earth is where we live, and is the only world we know, it can be a bit difficult to think of it as just one of the nine planets in the Sun's family – but that is what it is.

A view of our planet from space shows a world that is covered mainly in water, the blue of the oceans contrasting with a wide variety of different landscapes including deserts, mountainous regions and forests. A closer look, from a spacecraft orbiting the Earth, reveals examples of human activity, large towns and cities standing out as areas of grey against the natural background colors.

Life on our planet has evolved to suit the conditions here. We breathe the Earth's atmosphere and drink the water that was formed long ago in its history. From our vantage point in space we can see bright clouds of water vapour scurrying about high in the atmosphere. These clouds are just a part of the complex weather system that our planet enjoys. A look at the polar regions of the Earth will show that, here, water exists in solid form, as ice caps.

The Earth is the third planet out from the Sun. It is the largest of the four terrestrial planets, with a diameter of 7,928 miles. It orbits the Sun once every 365¼ days (one year) at an average distance of just around 93 million miles.

Like many of the other planets, the Earth has a varied and complex surface. There are many impact craters formed by meteorites, though a number of them are difficult to spot, having been eroded by the effects of wind and rain. On planets such as Mercury and the Moon, this kind of erosion has not occurred, because they have no appreciable atmosphere, and no weather.

Other types of feature on Earth include lofty mountain ranges, valleys and volcanoes. Indeed, the Earth contains more active volcanoes than any other of the major planets. However, the thing that makes Earth unique (as far as we are aware at the moment!) is that it is home to a wide and wonderful diversity of life, ranging from the simplest single-cell life forms through to man and whales, the Earth's two intelligent species. If we do find that we are not alone in space, and are eventually visited by an intelligent alien civilization, we can be sure that our planet will be of tremendous interest to them!

From orbit we look back as the Sun sets and a crescent Moon heralds in the night for the inhabitants of the beautiful and beckoning Earth below.

Because the Earth is rotating, and also because the Moon is moving through the sky, the Moon's shadow sweeps across the Earth's surface during a solar eclipse. Thus, from any point on the Earth's surface over which the shadow moves, an eclipse can only last a few minutes at most.

Solar eclipses are splendid sights and astronomers are prepared to travel many miles to see one. When the Sun's disc is completely covered, the sky becomes quite dark and the brighter stars become visible. The glow of the Sun's corona can be seen around the dark disc of the Moon, together with any large prominences which may be active at the time.

LUNAR ECLIPSES

The Earth also casts a shadow into space. If the Moon moves into this shadow, the sunlight that is illuminating the lunar surface is cut off, and the Moon is plunged into darkness. During a lunar eclipse, however, some sunlight is usually thrown on to the lunar surface by the Earth's atmosphere, giving the Moon a deep coppery-red colour.

During a lunar eclipse, the curved shadow of the Earth can be seen on the lunar surface. This shadow also has an umbra and a penumbra. If the Moon passes completely into the umbra, a total lunar eclipse takes place. A partial eclipse takes place when only part of the Moon passes through the umbra. Penumbral eclipses occur when the Moon only moves into the penumbra of the Earth. However, these eclipses are difficult to see because the Moon hardly gets any darker at all!

The Earth's shadow also has umbral and penumbral regions, as can be seen here in this diagram of a total lunar eclipse.

Lunar eclipses can be seen from anywhere on the side of the Earth facing the Moon at the time, although solar eclipses can only be seen from the limited area within the Moon's shadow. It follows from this that lunar eclipses are far more common than solar eclipses.

The Ancient Greeks noticed, in a lunar eclipse of the 4th century BC, that the Earth's shadow on the lunar surface was curved, proving that the Earth was spherical.

MARS

Mars is the fourth planet out from the Sun, orbiting it once every 687 days at an average distance of 136 million miles. It is only just over half the diameter of Earth, measuring almost 4,222 miles across. It appears red to us because of the huge amounts of dust scattered across its surface. These storms sometimes hide vast areas of the planet's surface – as happened in 1971 when the American Mariner 9 probe found it obscured for several weeks. Its red color led to Mars being named after the Roman god of war.

Mars has always been a popular target for astronomers, and is the only planet in the Solar System whose surface features are observable through Earth-based telescopes. One of these astronomers, the Italian Giovanni Schiaparelli, who created one of the biggest astronomical puzzles ever. In 1877, Schiaparelli noticed a number of markings on the planet which seemed to criss-cross the surface. He called these markings "canali", a word which means a natural channel (such as a stream or river). However, the word became wrongly translated as canals, which are artificial, and do not occur naturally!

It wasn't long before some astronomers decided that Mars was home to an intelligent civilization who had built the "canals" in order that water could be carried from the Martian polar ice caps (first discovered in 1666 by the Italian astronomer Giovanni Cassini) to irrigate the barren Martian deserts! Some astronomers, notably the American Percival Lowell, claimed to have discovered more canals, although their existence has now been finally disproved through the exploration of Mars by the many space probes that have visited the planet. The Martian polar ice caps do contain water, though we don't know how much.

By far the most successful probes to visit Mars were

The reddish color of the surface of Mars is clearly visible in this view looking across the Martian landscape.

the two American Viking probes. There were two Viking missions, both of which successfully landed on Mars in 1976. As well as the landers, there were two orbiters travelling around Mars. Between them, the Viking missions returned many thousands of photographs, including around 4,500 from the Martian surface. Lots of measurements were made of the Martian atmosphere and weather and a search for Martian life was made, although no life was found.

The surface of Mars contains many interesting features including the largest volcano in the Solar System, Olympus Mons. It is 15 miles high, its crater is 50 miles across, and the total diameter of its base is over 370 miles. There is also a spectacular system of valleys called Valles Marineris which straddles over 2,400 miles of the Martian equatorial region dwarfing such features as the Grand Canyon on Earth!

THE MINOR PLANETS

Also known as the asteroids, the minor planets are found mainly between the orbits of Mars and Jupiter, although a number have been found outside this region. Towards the end of the 18th century, it was thought that a planet orbited the Sun between Mars and Jupiter, and some astronomers set up an observing programme to try and locate the missing object. However, the first minor planet was found quite by accident on 1st January 1801 by the Italian astronomer Giuseppe Piazzi while he was observing stars in the constellation of Taurus from the Palermo Observatory in Sicily. He came across an object that didn't look like a star, and further observation eventually showed that it was a previously unseen body orbiting the Sun a little way beyond Mars.

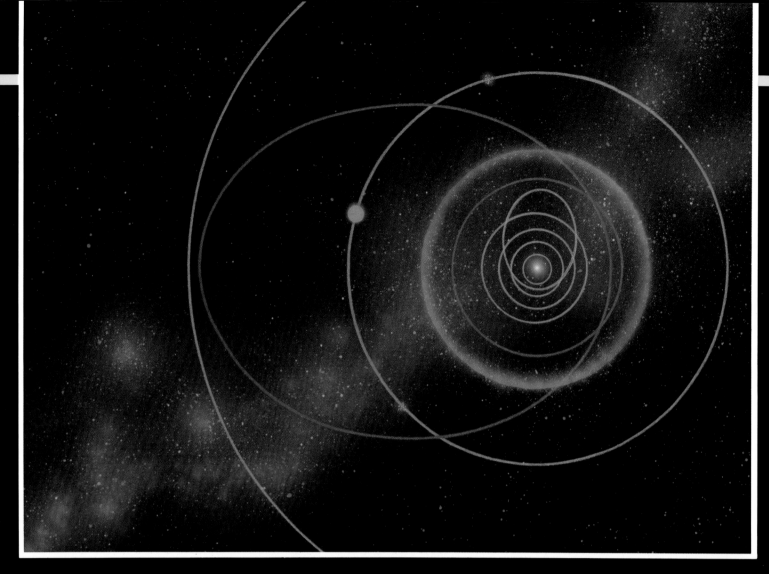

The new object was named Ceres, and it was very small by planetary standards. The search continued, and over the next few years, another three minor planets were discovered. The search was eventually considered complete and therefore abandoned in 1815. Yet, in 1845, a fifth minor planet was located, and not a year has gone by since then without further discoveries being made.

In all, around 3,500 minor planets have now been located and have had their orbits worked out. Astronomers think that there may be as many as a million! They range in size from Ceres, the largest, with a diameter of around 600 miles, down to tiny objects just a few yards across or even smaller. Even if all the minor planets were collected together, they would form an object smaller than the Moon. Yet it is becoming clear that the minor planets are interesting worlds. Many of the meteorites that land on the Earth (see Meteors and Meteorites, pages 24 and 25) are thought to have been formed by collisions between the minor planets, which knocked chunks of material off them.

Minor planets have been found well away from the main region. A number have orbits which carry them across the orbits of Mars and Earth, and some have made close approaches to our planet. The closest approach known took place in March 1989 when an

Although the main asteroid belt lies between the orbits of Mars and Jupiter, other asteroids travel around the Sun outside this region. These include the Trojans, located at two points along the orbital path of Jupiter, and the Apollo asteroids. The orbit of a typical Apollo asteroid is shown in yellow. The orbital path of Hidalgo, shown in red, takes it from the inner edge of the asteroid belt out to the orbit of Saturn.

object thought to be a few hundred yards in diameter came within 250 miles of us. This is a very small distance on the astronomical scale, and if the object had hit our planet, a great deal of damage and loss of life would have taken place. The speed of impact would have been somewhere in the region of 10 miles per second.

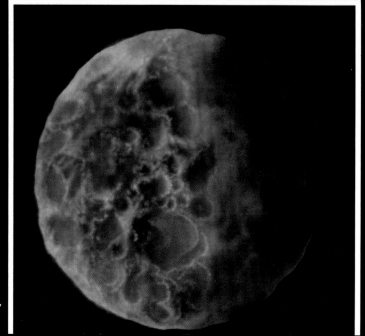

The surface of Ceres (shown here) and the other minor planets, are probably scarred with impact craters.

JUPITER

Jupiter is the largest planet in the solar system, with a diameter of 89,000 miles, over 11 times that of our planet. If it were hollowed out, nearly 1,500 Earths would fit inside. Jupiter travels around the Sun once every 11·86 years at an average distance of 483 million miles.

When we look at Jupiter even through a small telescope it appears as a yellowish flattened disc. This flattening is the result of the rapid rotation period of Jupiter, which is less than ten hours. Small telescopes also show details in the Jovian atmosphere. Particularly prominent are two dark belts which can be seen girdling Jupiter's equator. Larger telescopes show many more similar features including bright zones and darker belts. The zones are regions where gases are emerging from inside Jupiter to cool at the surface and the belts are regions where the gases are descending. The belts and zones display many colors including red, orange, brown and yellow.

Another prominent feature is the Great Red Spot, first seen by the Italian astronomer Giovanni Cassini in 1665, and observed almost continuously ever since. It is a huge oval atmospheric feature in Jupiter's southern hemisphere. It has changed in size and color in 300

The volcanically-active surface of the Jovian moon Io is visible below as we look out towards the giant planet Jupiter, Jupiter's faint ring system, invisible through Earth-based telescopes, can be seen as a narrow band girdling the planet.

years, and at times reaches a length of 25,000 miles, over three times the diameter of the Earth. It spins every six days or so, and a dark belt, which was not there in 1973 and 1974, was seen crossing it in 1979.

Jupiter has 16 satellites, the four largest of which (Io, Europa, Ganymede and Callisto), were discovered in 1610 by Galileo and are known as the Galilean satellites. The Voyager spacecraft sent back many pictures of these satellites. Io is volcanically active, and photographs showed plumes of material cast 175 miles above the surface. Callisto is the most heavily cratered world known; Europa has huge cracks in its surface; and Ganymede, 3,280 miles in diameter, is the largest satellite in the Solar System.

Jupiter has a faint ring system, invisible to Earth-based telescopes. It was discovered by the Voyager 1 craft in March 1979. The rings are only about half a mile thick and are made up of tiny particles. They reach to over 30,000 miles above the top of the Jovian atmosphere.

SATURN

Saturn is smaller than Jupiter, with a diameter of 75,000 miles. It is also flattened at the poles, again due to its rapid axial rotation. Saturn orbits the Sun once every 29½ years at an average distance of 886 million miles. It has belts and zones crossing its disc, and weighs more than all the other planets put together, except Jupiter, yet its density is less than that of water.

The most impressive feature of Saturn is its beautiful ring system. The rings are made up of millions of tiny particles and have three main sections, together with two dark divisions. The most conspicuous of these is the Cassini Division, discovered by Giovanni Cassini in 1675, which separates the two brightest rings. However, space probes have revealed other rings and have also shown that each of the main ring sections is actually made up of thousands of narrow ringlets and gaps.

Saturn has 21 satellites, the largest of which is Titan. Titan has a thick atmosphere which completely hides its surface from view. Its surface conditions are such that methane may exist as a gas, liquid or solid: methane rivers may drain into methane seas, methane snow may fall on methane-rich ice caps. The Cassini space probe, to be launched at the turn of the century, should give us more information about Titan. Saturn also has another six large satellites, the rest all being small, irregularly-shaped worlds.

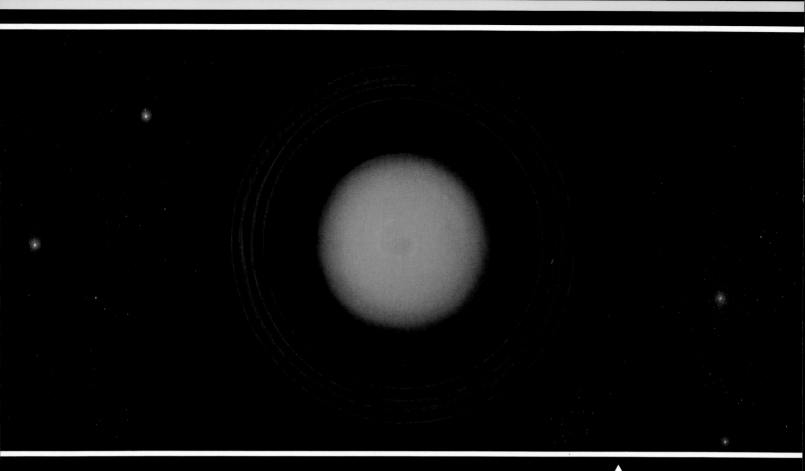

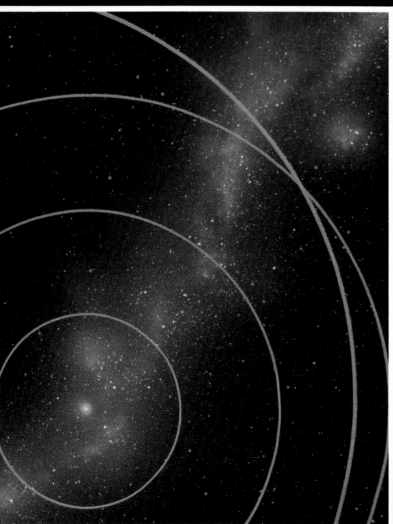

◀ The orbits of Saturn (inner), Uranus, Neptune and Pluto. It can be seen that for part of its journey around the Sun, the orbit of Pluto carries it within that of Neptune.

▲
The brightest of Uranus' rings are seen in this view looking down onto the planet's polar regions. The atmospheric features so prominent on Jupiter and Saturn are not nearly as well pronounced on Uranus. Some vague markings are visible here.

URANUS

Uranus is the seventh planet out from the Sun and was discovered quite accidentally by Sir William Herschel in 1781. Herschel was observing stars in Gemini when he spotted an object that looked very unstarlike in appearance. At first he thought he had discovered a comet, although once its orbit had been worked out it was found to be a planet. The discovery of Uranus was a milestone in astronomy as it was the first planet to be discovered with a telescope. The other planets known up to then – Mercury, Venus, Mars, Jupiter and Saturn – are all bright objects and easily visible to the unaided eye, and had been known since ancient times.

Uranus orbits the Sun once every 84 years at an average distance of 1,783 million miles. Its diameter is 31,570 miles. It has a very high axial tilt which means that the poles of the planet point alternately towards the Sun. For part of its orbit, the north pole is pointed at the Sun, and from this region on the planet the Sun appears high in the sky. As Uranus moves along its orbit, the Sun takes its place high over the Uranian equator following which the south pole is pointed at the Sun. From Earth we gaze down alternately on the polar regions and equator!

The visit of Voyager 2 in 1986 increased the number of known satellites orbiting Uranus from five to 15. The largest of the satellites is Titania, found by William Herschel in 1787, six years after he discovered Uranus itself. In the same year he discovered the satellite Oberon, which was followed by his discovery of Umbriel in 1802. The other two large satellites are Miranda and Ariel. Those discovered by Voyager are all quite small in comparison.

Voyager showed us that the largest satellites are fascinating worlds, especially Miranda, which was found to contain many different types of surface feature: craters were spotted together with valleys, cliffs and canyons – almost every type of feature seen elsewhere in the Solar System.

Valleys, faults and fractures were also seen on Titania, as were craters. Oberon also contains craters, although one of the most notable features seen on this satellite was a huge mountain estimated to tower around 12 miles above the surrounding landscape.

The darkest of the satellites was Umbriel, a world that is almost covered in craters. Its dark surface reflects very little of the sunlight it receives. Just where this dark material comes from remains a mystery. It may have come from inside the satellite itself or it may have fallen onto the surface from the Uranian ring system.

The rings of Uranus were discovered in 1977 when the planet was seen to pass in front of a star. Before the

Mountains and towering cliffs dominate the surface of Miranda, seen here with Uranus hovering over the horizon.

light from the star was blotted out by the planet itself, it was seen to "wink" five times. It was also seen to wink five times after the star emerged from behind Uranus. The only thing that could cause this would be a system of rings around the planet. These rings, although too faint to be seen from Earth, were able temporarily to hide the starlight from view as they passed over the star. The Voyager cameras brought the total number of known rings to eleven. These rings circle Uranus at between 10,500 and 16,500 miles above the planet's cloud tops.

Both Uranus and Neptune are faint and can only be usefully observed through a telescope or binoculars. Yet Uranus can actually become bright enough to be visible to the unaided eye, although you would have to know exactly where to look and the sky would have to be really dark, clear and moonless. Even through a telescope, however, Uranus appears as nothing more than a tiny greenish point of light. Neptune is visible as a pale bluish disc, again with no features visible. If observing either of these two planets seems to be a problem, Pluto is even harder to spot! Pluto is hundreds of times fainter than the faintest star visible to the unaided eye and very large telescopes are needed to reveal it at all!

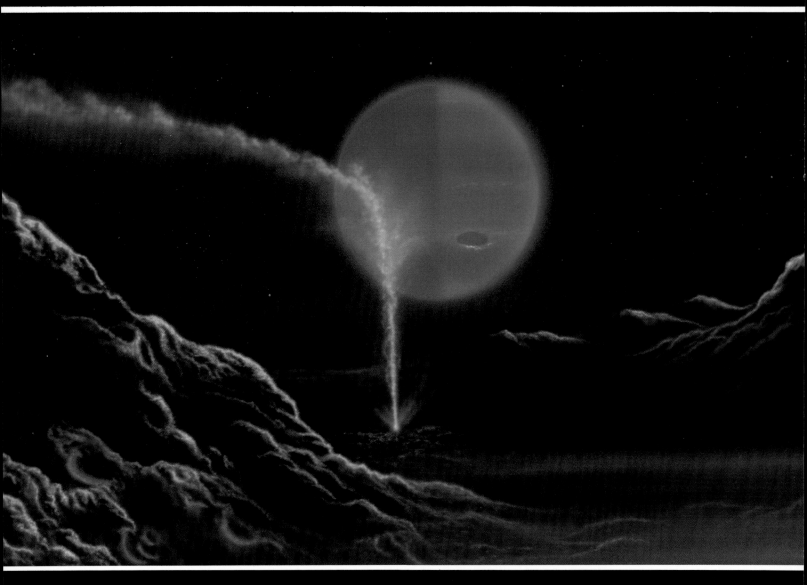

NEPTUNE

The blue disc of Neptune dominates the Triton skyline.

Neptune was discovered in 1846 by the German astronomers Johann Galle and Heinrich d'Arrest. It is the eighth planet out from the Sun and in some ways is a twin of Uranus, being only slightly smaller with a diameter of 30,200 miles. Neptune takes just under 165 years to orbit the Sun at a distance of 2,796 million miles. So far away is Neptune that the signals from the Voyager 2 space probe which flew past the planet in 1989 took over four hours to reach Earth.

The Voyager 2 cameras revealed bright polar collars and broad bands in different shades of blue girdling Neptune's southern hemisphere. Bright streaks of cirrus cloud were seen over the equatorial regions.

One of the numerous dark features seen by Voyager 2 was a huge oval storm cloud roughly the size of Earth and located to the south of the Neptunian equator. It was named the Great Dark Spot and is similar in many ways to the Great Red Spot on Jupiter. It rotates, and changed shape over a few days. Cirrus-type clouds of frozen methane formed and changed shape near it.

Voyager also photographed an area of frozen methane cirrus cloud, to the south of the Great Dark Spot, called the "Scooter", because it travelled faster than the other clouds.

Before Voyager 2 reached the planet, Neptune was thought to have only two satellites. Voyager discovered another six. The largest is Triton which has a diameter of 1,690 miles. Its surface contains many interesting features including craters, and features which looked very much like frozen lakes. These may have been formed by material being ejected from within Neptune which froze upon reaching the surface. It is thought by some scientists that Triton may be volcanically active, although this has yet to be confirmed.

Like the other three gas giant planets, Jupiter, Saturn and Uranus, Neptune has a system of rings. These were discovered by the Voyager cameras. This ring system is extremely faint, however, and cannot be seen through Earth-based telescopes. In all, three rings were seen around the planet together with a sheet of small particles seen extending through part of the main ring system.

PLUTO

Pluto was discovered in 1930 by the American astronomer Clyde Tombaugh after a long and very thorough search for a planet which was thought by astronomers to be orbiting the Sun beyond Neptune. The reason for this was that Neptune was seen to be wandering from its predicted orbit, and it was believed that the gravity from an as-yet undiscovered planet must have been tugging it off course.

Pluto is a very distant planet, orbiting the Sun once every 248 years at an average distance of almost 3,730 million miles. Its orbit is not circular and its distance from the the Sun varies considerably. For twenty years of its orbit, Pluto actually crosses the orbit of Neptune and so makes Neptune the most distant planet! This last happened in 1979, and until 1999 Pluto is travelling around the Sun inside the orbit of Neptune. Pluto is the smallest of the planets with a diameter thought to be around 1,430 miles. However, it is so small and far away that estimates of its diameter are very difficult to make.

Pluto has one satellite, Charon, which was discovered by the American astronomer James Christy in 1978. Charon is actually around half the diameter of Pluto itself which means that Pluto could be regarded as a double planet rather than a planet and satellite.

Just where Pluto and Charon came from isn't known with certainty. Some astronomers think that Pluto may once have been a satellite of Neptune and for some reason was pulled away from its parent planet into an orbit of its own. It is even thought by some that Pluto and Charon are chunks of material left over from the formation of the Solar System long ago, which never collected together to form a large planet. Pluto and Charon may be regarded as little more than distant asteroids. One thing is for certain. We have a great deal to learn about these dim and distant members of the Sun's family.

Astronauts of the future, when arriving at distant Pluto, will experience this view of the Pluto-Charon system. The orbital period of Charon is the same as Pluto's rotational period. This means that, for future observers located on the satellite-facing side of Pluto, Charon will be permanently visible in the Plutonian sky.

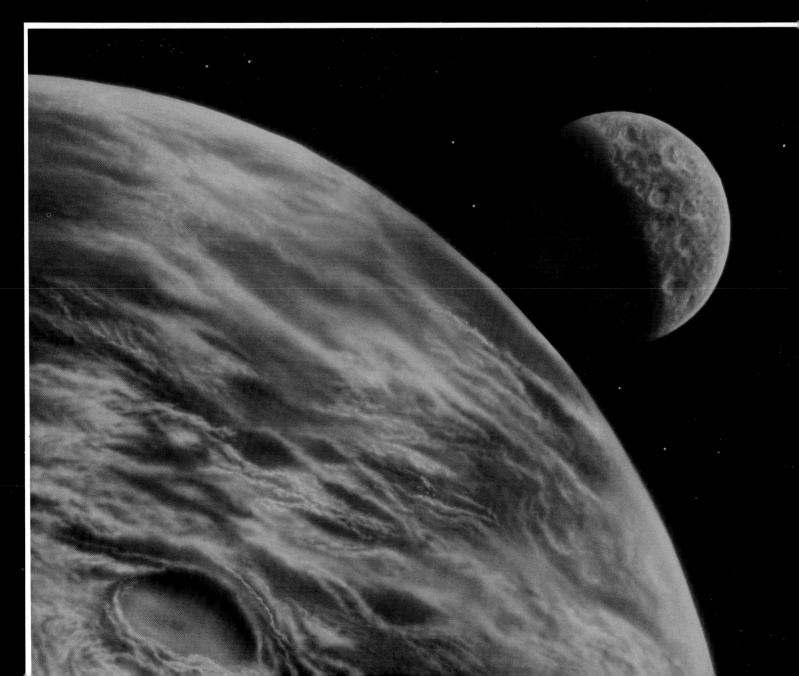

COMETS, METEORS AND METEORITES

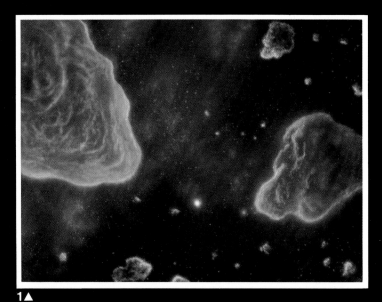

1▲

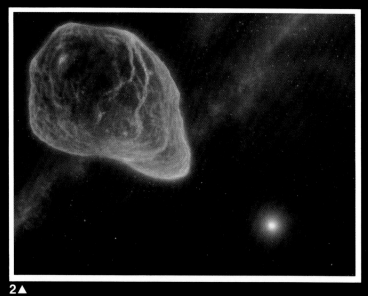

2▲

▼3

▼4

The cometary nuclei found within Oort's Cloud (1) sometimes escape and fall inwards towards the inner Solar System (2). Gradually, the Sun's heat begins to melt the material (3). This material, in the form of gas and dust, is blown away to form a coma and one or more tails (4).

COMETS

Comets are made up of ice and rocky material, rather like "dirty snowballs". A huge cloud of comets is thought to surround the solar system, beyond the orbit of Pluto. It is known as Oort's Cloud, after the Dutch astronomer, Jan Oort. Sometimes, a comet will fall from this cloud and start travelling towards us.

When a comet is a long way from the Sun, we can't see it because it is small and faint. However, as it gets closer, the heat from the Sun begins to melt the ice in the comet. A cloud of gas and dust, called the "coma", forms around the comet's head. Some of this material is then blown away to form one or more tails. As a comet rounds the Sun and begins to move away, the effects of the Sun's heat lessen. The tail disappears, followed by the coma, and the comet once more becomes faint.

One of the most famous comets is Halley's Comet which travels around the Sun once every 76 years. Like most comets, its orbit is long and narrow. Other comets have much shorter orbital periods. The shortest of all is that of Encke's Comet. This takes $3\frac{1}{3}$ years to go round the Sun. Others can take hundreds, or even thousands, of years to complete one orbit.

Some comets, such as Encke's Comet, have approached the Sun so many times that they have lost most of their material. When this happens there isn't enough left to form a tail, so all these comets are very small and faint.

METEORS AND METEORITES

As they travel around the Sun, comets leave particles of dust in their wakes, which eventually become spread out all along the path of the comet. At certain times of the year, the Earth passes through the orbital paths of certain comets. When this happens, particles from the comet enter the atmosphere at extremely high speeds and burn up. We see the destruction of the particles as streaks of light against the dark sky. These streaks of light, or meteors, are often referred to as shooting stars, although they are nothing to do with stars at all.

There have been many bright comets in our skies over the centuries. One of the brightest was the Great Daylight Comet of 1910.

The largest meteorite ever found weighs over 60 tons and is lying where it fell thousands of years ago at a place called Hoba West in South-West Africa. The second largest known meteorite is called the Ahnighito Meteorite and weighs just over 30 tons. This was found in Greenland by the American polar explorer Robert Edwin Peary in 1897. It is now in a museum in New York along with two other smaller meteorites found at the same time and in the same place.

SOME ACTIVE METEOR SHOWERS

NAME	DATE OF MAXIMUM ACTIVITY	DATES OF SHOWER ACTIVITY
Quadrantids	January 3/4	January 1-6
Perseids	August 11/12	July 25 - August 21
Orionids	October 21/22	October 16 - 30
Geminids	December 13/14	December 8 - 16

A meteor shower is named after the constellation in which its radiant lies. For example, the Perseids appear to radiate from a point in the constellation Perseus while the Geminid radiant lies close to Castor, one of the brightest stars in Gemini. The Quadrantids appear to radiate from a point in the sky that used to lie in an old constellation called Quadrans Muralis. This is a constellation which is no longer included on star charts, although the meteor shower named after it has kept its original name.

Billions of these tiny particles are scattered throughout the solar system, each orbiting the Sun rather like a tiny planet. They are far too small and faint to be seen unless they destroy themselves by entering the Earth's atmosphere and burning up, which they can do at any time and from any direction. The resulting meteors are called "sporadic" meteors. When the Earth passes through the orbital path of a comet we see a concentration of meteors called a "meteor shower."

During a meteor shower, the meteors all appear to come from the same point in the sky. This point is known as the radiant. If the tracks of shower meteors are plotted on a star chart, they all seem to converge at the same point. The Earth passes through certain swarms of particles at the same time each year, producing annual meteor showers. A list of the most active showers is included here.

Some particles entering the atmosphere are large enough to survive the fall and land on the ground. These objects are called meteorites, and many of them are thought to be broken-off chunks from the minor planets. Meteorite impacts can produce craters, rather like those on the Moon, and many such craters have been found. Although meteorites are fairly common, we don't know of anyone being killed by one, although there have been some near misses! If a large meteorite ever fell on a city, a great deal of damage could be done.

The idea of meteor radiants is well shown here, all the meteors appearing to emerge from a point in the sky to the lower right of picture.

THE LIFE OF A STAR

Stars are formed from nebulae (lower left), the energy released by nuclear reactions eventually blowing away any remaining gas and dust. The Sun will swell up into a red giant (upper right) and, once its nuclear fuel is depleted, a white dwarf (lower right).

STAR BIRTH

Stars are formed inside huge clouds of gas and dust. Particles of the cloud (called a nebula – see Star Clusters and Nebulae, page 30) collect together to produce clumps of material. More and more gas and dust falls onto these clumps making them larger and larger. Eventually, the clumps become such a size that the force of material pressing down results in their internal temperatures increasing. The temperature and pressure eventually reach such a point that nuclear reactions (similar to those which produce the Sun's light and heat – see The Sun, page 8) are started. The heat energy that is produced acts outwards, balancing out the force of gravity which would otherwise cause the clump to collapse. The clump then becomes stable, starts to radiate energy and becomes a star.

Some stars last much longer than others. Stars similar in size to the Sun will produce energy for around 10,000 million years, although stars which are much bigger will burn their hydrogen fuel at a much faster rate and may last for only a few tens of millions of years or so.

RED GIANTS

There comes a time when the store of hydrogen fuel at the core of the star is used up. When this happens, changes take place within the star. The decrease in the amount of heat energy being produced means that the force of gravity becomes once more dominant. The star will again start to compress which will result in the temperature and pressure at the core increasing. Eventually, conditions will be such that the helium formed by the crushing together of hydrogen will itself be changed into another element. Nuclear reactions start again and the new production of heat forces the outer layers of the star to expand. It grows to many times its original size, and its outer layers cool and it turns into what astronomers call a red giant. Aldebaran, the brightest star in Taurus (see Star Charts – Northern Winter, page 42) is a typical red giant.

WHITE DWARFS

Eventually, of course, the store of helium fuel runs out and the core of the star once more becomes compressed. For stars like the Sun, there will be no further nuclear reactions and gravity will take over, eventually compressing the star into a super-dense object called a white dwarf. Stars which are much larger than the Sun will carry on producing nuclear reactions, converting each successive element into another.

As the star cools and compresses, heat pressure from the core can force the outer layers away into interstellar space to form a planetary nebula (see Star Clusters and Nebulae). The formation of a planetary nebula heralds the formation of a white dwarf.

The Sun will eventually turn into a white dwarf. The tremendous pull of gravity will compress the central regions of the Sun (and stars of similar size) into an incredibly dense object. The effect is similar in some ways to the compression of snow into a snowball and, if pressure is continued, into a ball of ice. A white dwarf is around a million times as dense as water, so tightly is the material in it packed together. A teaspoonful of white dwarf material would weigh many tons.

NEUTRON STARS

Stars that are much more massive than the Sun continue to produce energy by continuing to undergo nuclear reactions. Eventually, however, they suffer the same fate as those similar to the Sun. However, these stars are so huge that they are crushed to form even denser objects than white dwarfs. They form instead what we call neutron stars, and a teaspoonful of neutron star material would weigh millions of tons. If the Earth could somehow be squashed to the same density, all the matter forming our planet would be crushed to the size of a large marble.

Blue-White supergiant stars (left) are among the hottest and most massive stars known. These massive stars end their lives in a huge explosion called a supernova (right). Most of its material is ejected into surrounding space, leaving the core to collapse into either a neutron star or a collapsed star at the center of a black hole.

Although we can't actually SEE a black hole, astronomers think they have located a number of these fascinating objects by examining violent bursts of X-rays emitted as material is dragged from a companion star (such as the red giant seen here) into an orbiting black hole. As this happens, the gas is violently heated up and gives off X-ray energy. ▶

BLACK HOLES

The most massive stars of all are crushed beyond the white dwarf and neutron star stages. The gravitational compression force of these stars is totally irresistible, and the material in them is squashed to its limits.

The escape velocity of the Earth is almost seven miles per second. In other words, in order to escape the pull of Earth's gravity, a spaceship would have to travel at almost seven miles per second. The escape velocity of a white dwarf is around 1,850 miles per second! Imagine

VARIABLE STARS

The light from the Sun is constant and doesn't alter. However, there are many stars which vary in brightness over periods of time. These stars are known as variable stars and there are two main types.

Some variable stars change in brightness because of changes taking place within the star itself. In many cases the star expands and contracts, so increasing and decreasing in brightness as it does so. These regular changes in size are known as pulsations. There are a number of different types of pulsating variable star, each with its own basic appearances. Some variables have been seen to change over only a few hours or even less, while others take months or even years to complete a sequence of brightness variations. The latter are known as long-period variables, and they are all red giant stars.

The other type of variable star is that where the variations in brightness are caused by a darker, fainter star orbiting a brighter one. If the orbits of the stars around each other are lined up with Earth, the fainter star will occasionally pass in front of the brighter one thereby blotting out part of its light from us. The star will seem to dim for a time until the fainter star "moves out of the way".

Some stars (although perhaps not classed as proper variables) are seen to suddenly increase in brightness before fading back once more. These stars are called novae and they can appear at any time and in any direction in the sky. Stars which may be very faint can erupt to become bright enough to be seen with the unaided eye. Stars which become novae are members of binary (or double) star systems where one of the stars is actually a white dwarf. Such is the strength of the gravity from the white dwarf that it pulls material away from its companion. This material falls onto the surface of the white dwarf and builds up until the temperature and pressure at its base become so high that nuclear reactions (like those in the Sun) are triggered. These reactions are enough to throw all the material that has built up out into space, so producing an explosion and a temporary increase in the star's brightness. Some novae have been seen to erupt only once, although some have brightened up on several occasions.

Some extremely young stars display erratic variations in brightness. These variations are thought to be caused by instabilities in the young star which is still in the process of formation. These so-called T Tauri stars are often enveloped inside clouds of material, some of which is ejected by the star itself.

DOUBLE STARS

Our Sun is a solitary star, its only companions being the collection of planets, comets and other objects orbiting it. However, most stars are actually members of star systems which contain anything from two to several hundred individual stars (see Star Clusters and Nebulae, page 30).

Lots of stars are members of double star systems, pairs of stars which are moving together through space, held together by their combined gravitational attraction. Some double stars actually orbit each other. These stars are called binary stars, and their orbital periods vary from less than an hour to thousands of years.

However, not all stars which appear to be close together in space are actually members of a double star system. If two stars happen to lie in more or less the same line of sight as seen from Earth, they may seem to be next to each other, although one could be a great deal further away. These stars are known as optical doubles, their appearance as doubles being an optical illusion. A similar effect is seen on Earth if you stand looking at street lights. By lining two up with each other, they may seem to be close together, although one will be further away from you.

To the inhabitants of a planet orbiting a double star system, the daytime sky would be a wonderful spectacle, with twin suns shining down! Here we see an imaginary view from the surface of a planet orbiting the yellow and blue components of the double star Albireo in the constellation of Cygnus (see Summer Stars Looking South).

MULTIPLE STARS

Some stars are members of multiple star systems, in which several stars are linked together by their mutual gravitational attraction. The bright star Alpha Centauri is a good example of a multiple star. A small telescope will show that Alpha Centauri is a double star. The two individual stars orbit each other once every 80 years, making it a binary star system. However, large telescopes reveal another star quite close by. This star, called Proxima Centauri, is a little closer to us than the main pair, and is the closest star to the Earth. Proxima Centauri is thought to orbit the main Alpha Centauri pair every half a million years or so, making Alpha Centauri a triple star system.

Some multiple star systems contain even more stars, all of which move around one another in complicated orbits. Imagine how the sky would appear from Earth if the Sun were a member of such a system!

STAR CLUSTERS AND NEBULAE

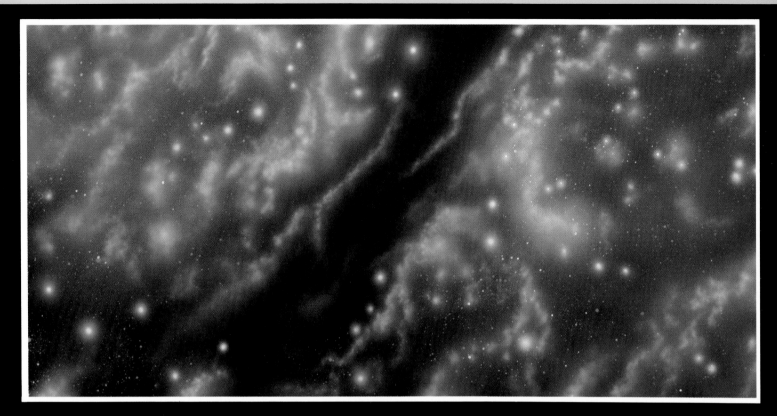

STAR CLUSTERS

Most stars are members of huge clusters which can contain many thousands of individual members.

There are two types of star cluster. Open or galactic clusters are random collections of stars with no definite shape, which contain anything from around a dozen to several hundred stars. They are found within the main plane of our Milky Way Galaxy. Over a thousand open clusters have been identified, one of the most famous of which is the Pleiades cluster in Taurus, the Bull. The Pleiades cluster is formed of young, hot stars and is a splendid sight in binoculars. On photographs taken with large telescopes traces of dust and gas can be seen scattered throughout the cluster. This is all that remains of the original nebula out of which the star cluster was formed.

The Pleiades – or Seven Sisters, because seven stars can be seen with the naked eye – at just over 400 light years away, is one of the closest open clusters.

The famous Ring Nebula in the constellation of Lyra.

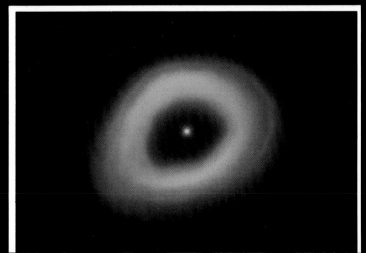

Globular clusters are spherical or globe-shaped collections of stars. They are much bigger than the open clusters and are found outside the Milky Way Galaxy. A typical globular cluster contains several tens of thousands of stars. These stars are generally much older than those found in open clusters.

There are one or two globular clusters visible to the naked eye, one of the most famous being Omega Centauri in the southern constellation of Centaurus. It was first mentioned by astronomers 2,000 years ago and, until telescopes were turned towards it in the 17th century, had always been taken to be a star.

It isn't only our own Galaxy that contains clusters. Many other galaxies have also been seen to contain open and globular clusters. The Andromeda Spiral has many globular clusters around it and its spiral arms play host to large numbers of open clusters.

NEBULAE

Nebulae are vast clouds of dust and gas seen throughout the spiral arms of the Milky Way. The word "nebula" comes from an old word meaning mist, cloud or vapour. Just as there is more than one type of star cluster, so there are several different types of nebula.

Emission nebulae are those which contain very hot stars. The energy from these stars is so immense that the gas in the nebula is actually made to shine and emit its own light. The Orion Nebula in Orion is one of the best examples of an emission nebula. The huge multiple star Theta Orionis throw off vast amounts of energy deep within the Orion Nebula causing the gas to shine. Emission nebulae are reddish in color.

Reflection nebulae show up because they reflect the light from nearby stars which are not hot enough to make the cloud shine. Instead, the particles of dust in the nebula reflect the starlight, and are seen as a blue color. The dust and gas surrounding the stars in the Pleiades is reflection nebulosity.

Dark nebulae are clouds of dark material which contain no stars and which simply blot out the light from stars beyond. In many respects they resemble huge "holes in the sky" and for many years this is what they were thought to be. One of the best examples of a dark nebula is the Coal Sack nebula in Crux. The Coal Sack lies around 500 light years away and was first spotted by Portugese sailors, who referred to it as a vast blot of matter obscuring the star clouds of the southern Milky Way.

OTHER TYPES OF NEBULA

There are two other types of nebula, although they are not true nebulae in the strict sense of the word. Planetary nebulae are shells of gas thrown off by stars which are about to collapse to form white dwarfs. They are seen as discs of light and, in many ways, resemble the appearance through telescopes of the outer gaseous planets in our Solar System, hence the name planetary nebulae. Hundreds of planetary nebulae are known, one of the most famous being the Ring nebula in Lyra. The hot surface of its central star, revealed as it shed its outer layers into space, emits energy which causes the gas in the surrounding planetary nebula to shine.

Supernova remnants are huge clouds of material thrown off as massive stars end their lives in colossal explosions which we call supernovae. The outer layers of the star are blown into space while the core of the star collapses to form a neutron star or black hole. One of the most famous examples is the Crab Nebula in

The bright globular cluster 47 Tucanae together with the outer edge of the Small Magellanic Cloud (SMC).

Taurus. This expanding cloud of gas is all that remains of the outer layers of a star that was seen to explode in AD1054. At the point at which the explosion took place, deep within the Crab Nebula, a neutron star has been revealed by telescopes. Other supernova remnants have been spotted, some of which are the result of supernova explosions which took place many thousands of years ago. The Veil Nebula in Cygnus is a huge gaseous loop still expanding into space after a supernova explosion 35,000 years ago.

This view of the central region of the Pleiades open star cluster reveals traces of the nebulosity from which the stars in the cluster were formed.

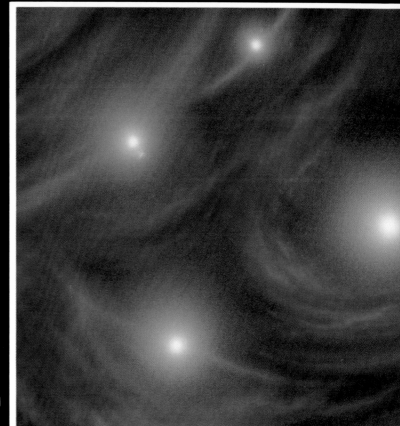

THE MILKY WAY GALAXY

On a dark, clear night a faint misty band of light may be seen stretching across the sky. This is the Milky Way, a huge spiral-shaped collection of around 100,000 million stars, mixed with interstellar gas and dust. The combined light of the stars – most of which are too faint to be seen with the unaided eye – gives a pearly glow, though this is broken up in places by huge clouds of dark nebulosity which blot out light from the stars beyond them. Our Sun is part of the Milky Way Galaxy.

As long as 2,000 years ago people began wondering if the Milky Way might be made up of the combined light of many stars, but this wasn't confirmed until Galileo studied it with a telescope in 1609-10. Over the years the Milky Way has featured in many myths and legends, including those of the Norsemen, who believed it was the Path of Ghosts going to Valhalla, the palace of their heroes killed in battle.

There are three main sections to the Milky Way Galaxy. There is a huge central bulge of old stars with very little gas and dust. The disc of the Galaxy surrounds the central bulge and contains a number of spiral arms, giving the Galaxy the appearance of a colossal catherine wheel suspended in space. Our Sun lies between two of the spiral arms, roughly two-thirds of the way out from the centre. The final part is the galactic halo, a huge spherical gathering of stars which completely surrounds the central bulge and extends out to around 50,000 light years. Most of the stars in the halo are contained within globular clusters (see Star Clusters and Nebulae, page 30) which travel around the center of the Galaxy in elongated, and very long orbits. This is in contrast to the stars and star clusters in the disc which orbit the centre in paths which are nearly circular. Those stars nearer the center have much shorter orbits than those further out. The Sun takes around 225 million years to travel around the galactic center.

The Milky Way Galaxy is huge. Its total diameter is around 100,000 light years and the disc is about 3,000 light years thick. The thickness of the central bulge is 10,000 light years and its diameter some 20,000 light years. Yet, large as it is, there are other galaxies which are much larger.

From a location above the galactic disc, we are presented with a spectacular view looking across the spiral arms of our Milky Way Galaxy.

A view looking across the arms and nucleus of the Andromeda Spiral Galaxy in the direction of our own Milky Way Galaxy, visible in the background.

THE LOCAL GROUP

Our Galaxy is a member of a cluster of galaxies which we call the Local Group. There are around 30 galaxies in the Local Group, the largest of which is the Andromeda Spiral, a huge system similar in shape to our own Galaxy, although it is about half as large again. The Andromeda Spiral lies just over two million light years away and is the most distant object visible to the unaided eye (see Star Charts for Northern Autumn, page 40). Most of the other galaxies in the Local Group are small systems, quite unlike either the Milky Way Galaxy or the Andromeda Spiral in appearance.

Wide field view showing the Large (left) and Small Magellanic Clouds.

OTHER GALAXIES AND CLUSTERS OF GALAXIES

There are two main types of galaxy: the spirals (described above) and the ellipticals. Elliptical galaxies can vary in shape from being almost spherical (resembling huge globular clusters) to highly stretched out, or elongated. Some of the largest galaxies known are ellipticals. There are also irregular galaxies which have no really well-defined shape. The two best-known examples of irregular galaxies are the Large and Small Magellanic Clouds. These are visible high in the southern sky and are the closest galaxies to our own, lying at distances of less than 200,000 light years, only a tenth of the distance to the Andromeda Spiral.

Many other groups of galaxies are known. Some of these are quite small with only a few member galaxies. In all, there are about 50 groups of galaxies within 50 million light years of the Local Group.

Even larger than the groups of galaxies are the clusters, some of which have hundreds or even thousands of members. The closest of these is the Virgo Cluster, between 40 and 70 million light years away. Over 2,000 individual galaxies have been photographed in the Virgo Cluster, though there may be many more dwarf galaxies too faint to photograph.

The Virgo Cluster lies at the centre of a huge collection of galaxies called the Local Supercluster. Superclusters are made up of many different clusters and groups of galaxies, and their diameters can be up to tens of millions of light years in size. The Local Group lies near the edge of the Local Supercluster.

THE FUTURE

Space exploration will also develop and grow. At the moment we are busy sending out probes to explore the other planets and satellites in the Solar System, although eventually probes will be despatched to other stars beyond our region of space. The main problem here is the vast distances that such interstellar probes will have to cover. Scientists will have to invent better types of propulsion for these probes before such a mission could take place. The Pioneer and Voyager probes, which between them explored the four gas giant planets Jupiter, Saturn, Uranus and Neptune, are currently heading out of the Solar System, although it will be many thousands of years before they pass anywhere near another star!

Still, who knows what the next few decades will bring? Space exploration has progressed remarkably over the last twenty years or so, and it may not be long before we despatch our first probes to the stars....

An interstellar probe approaches the magnificent Cone Nebula on a journey of exploration far beyond the confines of our Solar System.

Telescopes of the future will be sited on the Moon, allowing us to study the sky without having to peer through the Earth's murky atmosphere.

Astronomy has certainly come a long way from when early stargazers first looked up at the sky with no real idea as to what they were looking at. What were to them nothing more than points or smudges of light in the night sky have been revealed as stars, nebulae, galaxies and other fascinating objects. Through the use of modern, gigantic telescopes we have been able to peer further and further into space. Yet we still have a long way to go before we finally unlock all the secrets of the Universe.

Earth-based astronomers are unfortunate in that they have to look at the stars through the atmosphere, which absorbs some of the already-faint light reaching us. The launch of the Hubble Space Telescope in 1990 was a major step forward in astronomical research. For the first time, a large telescope has been placed in orbit above the obscuring effects of the Earth's atmosphere and this fine instrument promises to reveal much that we don't know about the sky and the wonders it holds.

But what about further into the future? Telescopes and observatories will eventually be placed on other members of the Solar System. Lunar observatories will probably be established by the early part of the 21st century. The Moon has no atmosphere to blot out the light from distant and faint stars and galaxies and is therefore an ideal place to house an astronomical observatory.

LOCATING THE POLE STAR

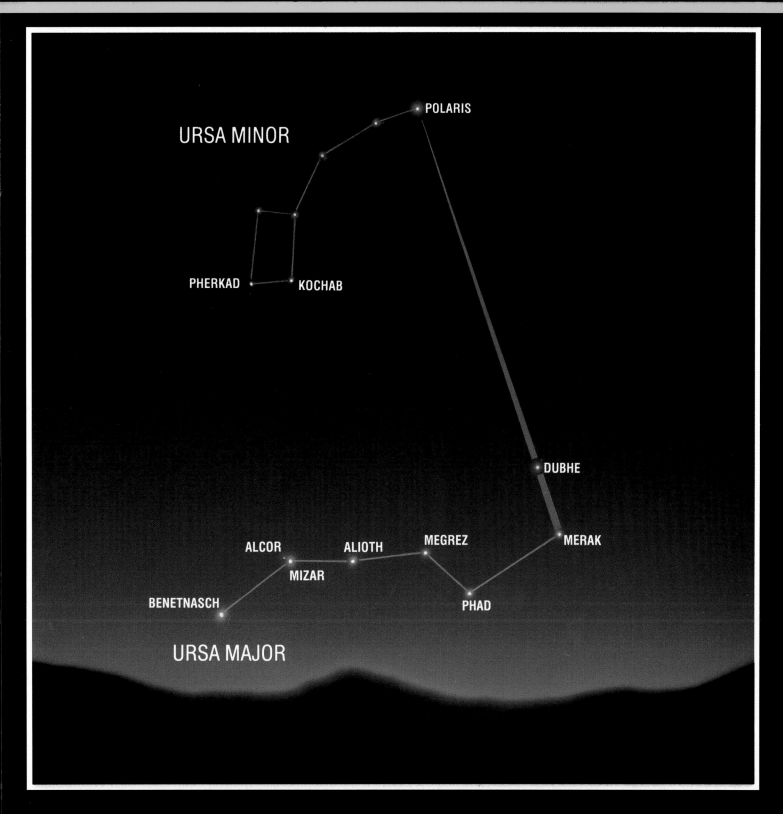

The constellation of Ursa Major (the Great Bear) is quite large and faint, although its seven brightest stars are arranged in a conspicuous pattern. We call this pattern the Plough.

Merak and Dubhe, the pair of stars at the end of the Plough, are often referred to as the "Pointers". An imaginary line from Merak through Dubhe as shown will lead you to Polaris, the Pole Star. This is the leading star of the constellation Ursa Minor (the Little Bear).

Polaris marks the position of the North Celestial Pole. The axis of the Earth is pointed towards this star. As the

Earth spins, and the stars appear to rise and set, the Pole Star stays still, with all the other stars appearing to travel around it. If you were at the north pole, the Pole Star would be directly overhead. If you find the Pole Star, you will be looking towards the north.

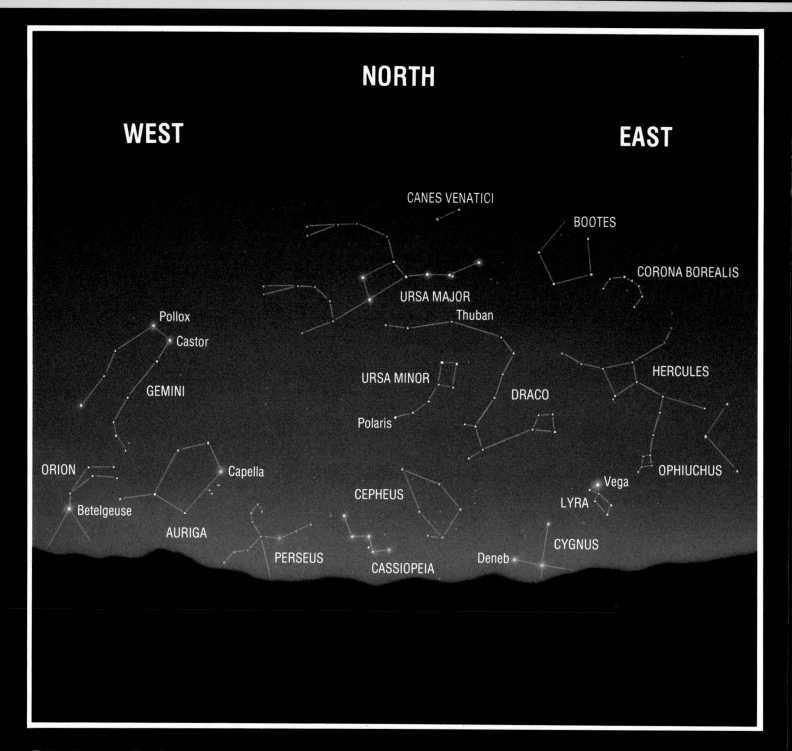

NORTH

WEST

EAST

CANES VENATICI

BOOTES

CORONA BOREALIS

URSA MAJOR

Thuban

Pollox

Castor

GEMINI

URSA MINOR

HERCULES

DRACO

Polaris

ORION

Capella

OPHIUCHUS

Betelgeuse

CEPHEUS

Vega

AURIGA

LYRA

PERSEUS

CASSIOPEIA

Deneb

CYGNUS

SPRING STARS
looking north

During spring, the sprawling constellation Ursa Major (the Great Bear) is located high overhead. The prominent pattern of its seven brightest stars make up the familiar Plough. As we have seen, the two stars at the end of the "bowl" of the Plough, furthest away from the Plough "handle", can be used to locate Polaris, the Pole Star.

Continuing the line of the Pointers beyond Polaris leads us to the prominent "W" of Cassiopeia, located low over the northern horizon. In six months' time the Plough and Cassiopeia will have exchanged positions. Cassiopeia will occupy the overhead point while the Plough will be skimming the northern horizon. Looking towards the south we see the distinctive shape of Leo (the Lion) striding across the sky. Other prominent groups include Bootes (the Herdsman) and Virgo (the Virgin), their

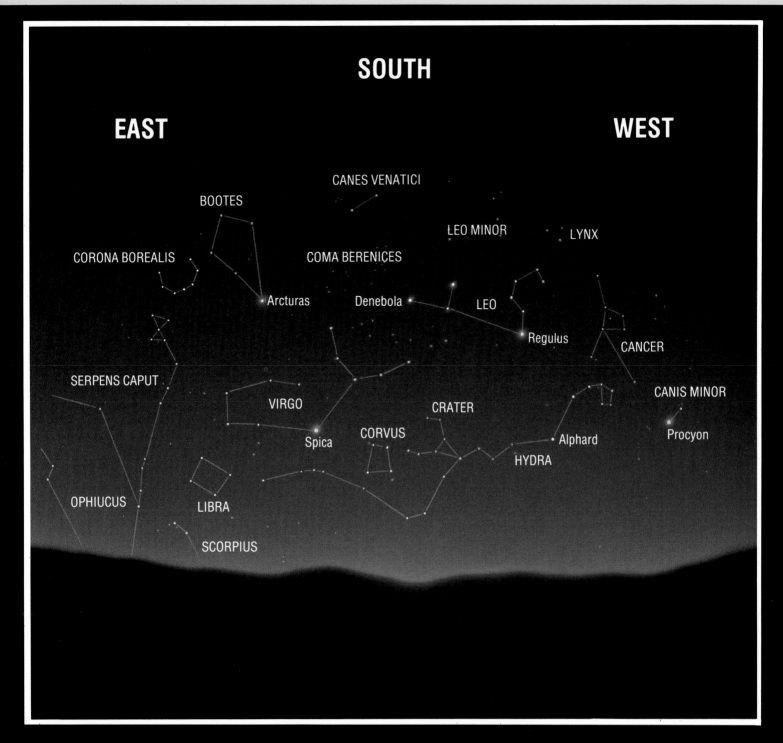

SOUTH

EAST

WEST

CANES VENATICI

BOOTES

LEO MINOR

LYNX

CORONA BOREALIS

COMA BERENICES

Arcturas

Denebola

LEO

Regulus

CANCER

SERPENS CAPUT

CANIS MINOR

VIRGO

CRATER

Spica

CORVUS

Alphard

Procyon

OPHIUCUS

HYDRA

LIBRA

SCORPIUS

leading stars Arcturus and Spica standing out well.

The winter constellations Gemini (the Twins) and Orion are disappearing over the western horizon, not to become prominent again until the following winter. On the other hand, the sight of Lyra (the Lyre) and its leading star Vega climbing up from the eastern horizon heralds the forthcoming summer when Vega and the other summer constellations will take their place high in the southern sky.

SPRING STARS
looking south

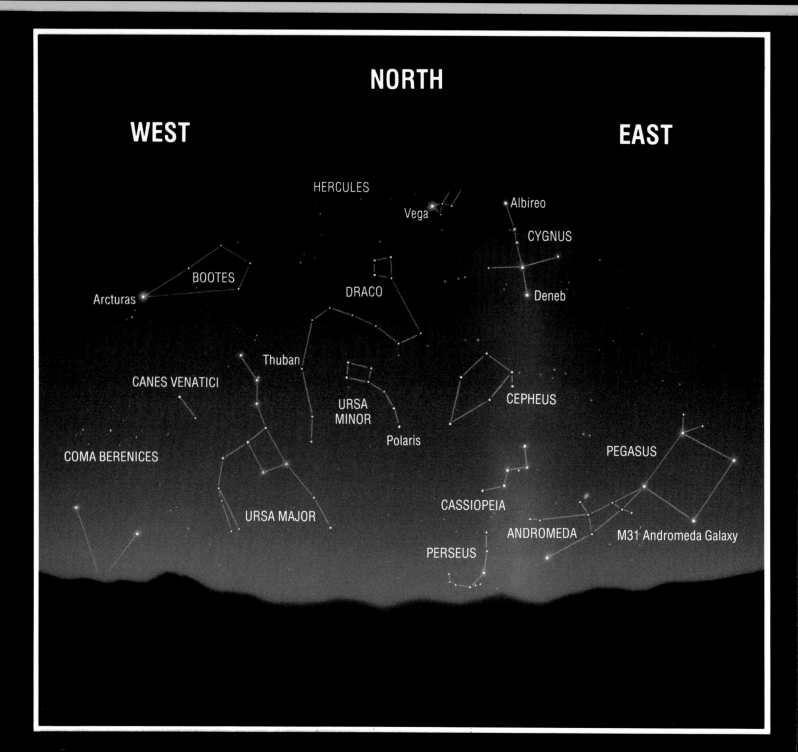

NORTH

WEST

EAST

HERCULES

Albireo

Vega

CYGNUS

BOOTES

DRACO

Deneb

Arcturas

Thuban

CANES VENATICI

URSA
MINOR

CEPHEUS

Polaris

COMA BERENICES

PEGASUS

URSA MAJOR

CASSIOPEIA

M31 Andromeda Galaxy

ANDROMEDA

PERSEUS

SUMMER STARS
looking north

Summer sees the Plough in the northwestern sky, slowly making its way towards its autumn position over the northern horizon. Cassiopeia is climbing in the east and will be prominent overhead in a few months' time. As with the other spring groups, Leo (the Lion) has dipped out of sight in the west while Pegasus and Andromeda are beginning their rise out of the eastern sky.

Vega is now high overhead and forming the conspicuous Summer Triangle with Deneb (in Cygnus) and Altair (in Aquila). These three stars are the first to appear as summer nights set in and are an unmistakable group high in the southern sky. The Milky Way runs from Cassiopeia in the east right overhead and on down through the Summer Triangle. This whole area is rich in stars and star fields and is well worth sweeping with

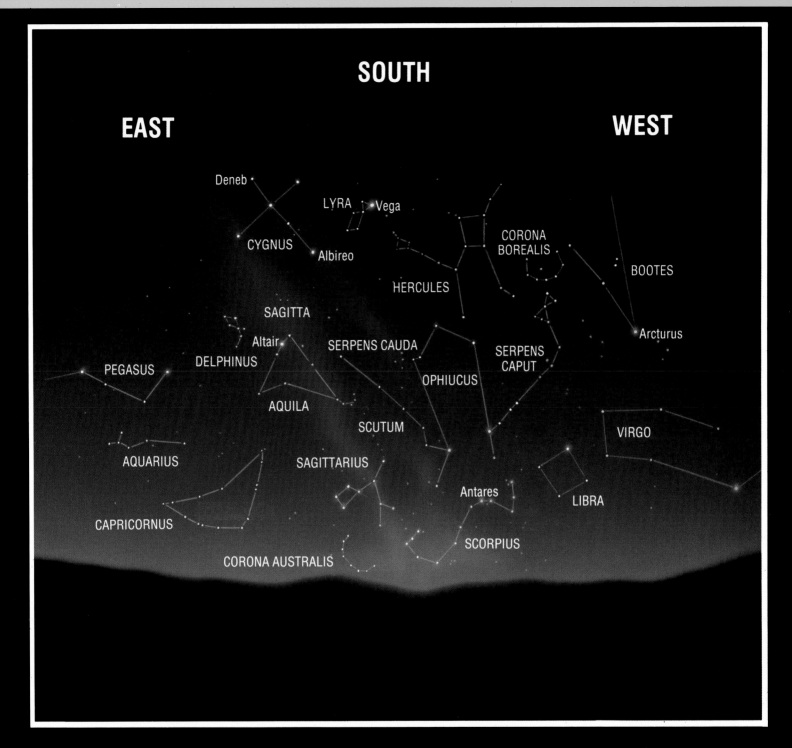

SOUTH

EAST

WEST

Deneb
LYRA · Vega
CYGNUS
Albireo
CORONA
BOREALIS
HERCULES
BOOTES
SAGITTA
Altair
SERPENS CAUDA
DELPHINUS
SERPENS
CAPUT
Arcturus
PEGASUS
OPHIUCUS
AQUILA
SCUTUM
VIRGO
AQUARIUS
SAGITTARIUS
Antares
LIBRA
CAPRICORNUS
SCORPIUS
CORONA AUSTRALIS

binoculars or a small telescope. Look out also for the large but somewhat dim constellation of Hercules, closely attended by Corona Borealis (the Northern Crown).

Low down above the southern horizon can be seen Antares, the leading star of the constellation Scorpius (the Scorpion). Mist or cloud may tend to hide Antares from view, although given clear skies, its ruddy glow is quite distinctive. A useful pointer to Antares is to extend the line joining Deneb and Albireo in Cygnus for a distance equal to around three times the length of Cygnus.

SUMMER STARS
looking south

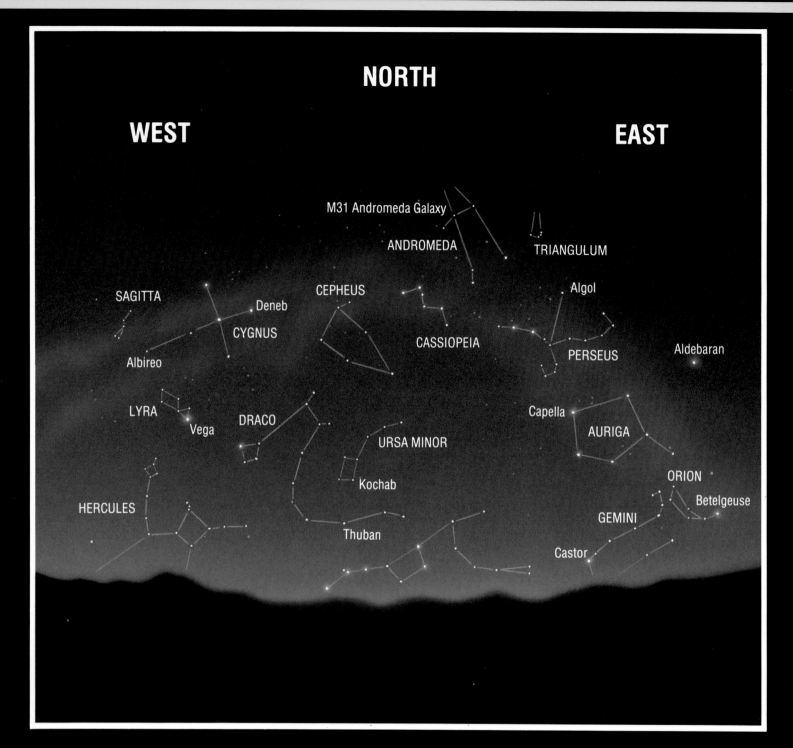

NORTH

WEST

EAST

M31 Andromeda Galaxy

ANDROMEDA

TRIANGULUM

SAGITTA

Deneb

CEPHEUS

Algol

CYGNUS

CASSIOPEIA

PERSEUS

Aldebaran

Albireo

LYRA

DRACO

Vega

URSA MINOR

Capella

AURIGA

Kochab

ORION

HERCULES

Betelgeuse

GEMINI

Thuban

Castor

AUTUMN STARS
looking north

With the passing of summer, the Summer Triangle is now making its way out of our view towards the western horizon. Its place of prominence in the southern sky is now occupied by Pegasus and Andromeda. The autumn night sky is something of a "watery" place, playing host to the long and winding constellation of Pisces (the Fishes) extending around the east and south of Pegasus. Also in evidence are Cetus (the Whale), Aquarius (the Water Bearer), Piscis Austrinus (the Southern Fish) and Capricornus (the Sea Goat). We even have Delphinus (the Dolphin) following the Summer triangle out to the west and Eridanus (the River) coming up in the east!

Fomalhaut, the brightest star in Piscis Austrinus, can be seen low over the southern horizon during autumn evenings. A useful direction finder to this star is to follow

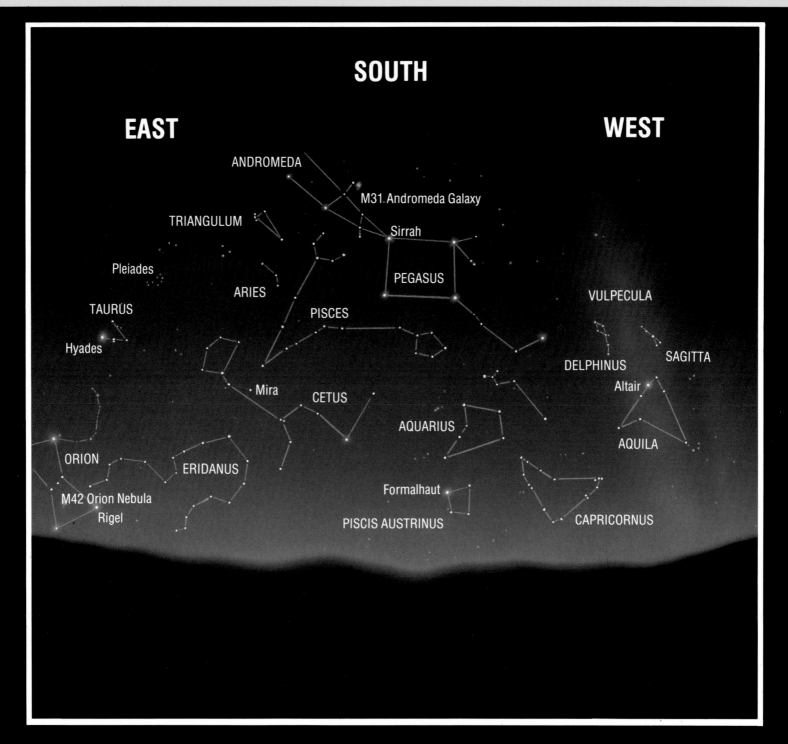

SOUTH

EAST

WEST

ANDROMEDA

M31 Andromeda Galaxy

TRIANGULUM

Sirrah

PEGASUS

Pleiades

VULPECULA

ARIES

PISCES

TAURUS

SAGITTA

Hyades

DELPHINUS

Mira

Altair

CETUS

ORION

AQUARIUS

AQUILA

ERIDANUS

M42 Orion Nebula

Formalhaut

Rigel

CAPRICORNUS

PISCIS AUSTRINUS

the line formed by the two stars on the west side of the Square of Pegasus down towards the south. Fomalhaut is the first and only bright star you meet.

Over to the east, Capella in Auriga is once more rising towards what will be its dominant position high in the winter night sky. Below it, and also rising to approaching prominence, is Orion, Taurus (the Bull) and Gemini (the Twins). The sight of Orion in the eastern sky tells of the cold winter evenings to come!

AUTUMN STARS
looking south

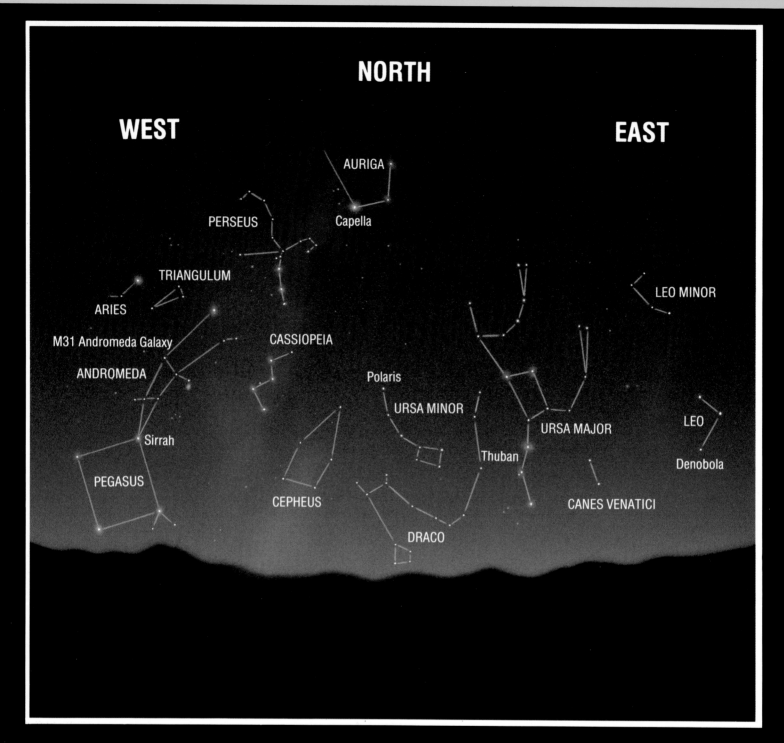

NORTH

WEST

EAST

AURIGA

Capella

PERSEUS

LEO MINOR

TRIANGULUM

ARIES

M31 Andromeda Galaxy

CASSIOPEIA

ANDROMEDA

Polaris

URSA MINOR

LEO

Sirrah

URSA MAJOR

Denobola

PEGASUS

Thuban

CEPHEUS

CANES VENATICI

DRACO

WINTER STARS
looking north

The winter sky is ruled by the mighty Orion, standing high in the south and closely attended by Canis Major (the Great Dog) and Canis Minor (the Small Dog) as he chases Lepus (the Hare) along the banks of the river Eridanus. Sirius, the brightest member of Canis Major, is unmistakable in the southern sky. There are more bright stars in the winter night sky than at any other time of the year. Orion, splendid enough in itself, is surrounded by a large circular pattern of bright stars formed by Sirius, Procyon (in Canis Minor), Castor and Pollux (in Gemini), Capella (situated overhead in Auriga) and Aldebaran (in Taurus).

Over to the west, Pegasus and Andromeda are disappearing out of view while in the east we can see Leo

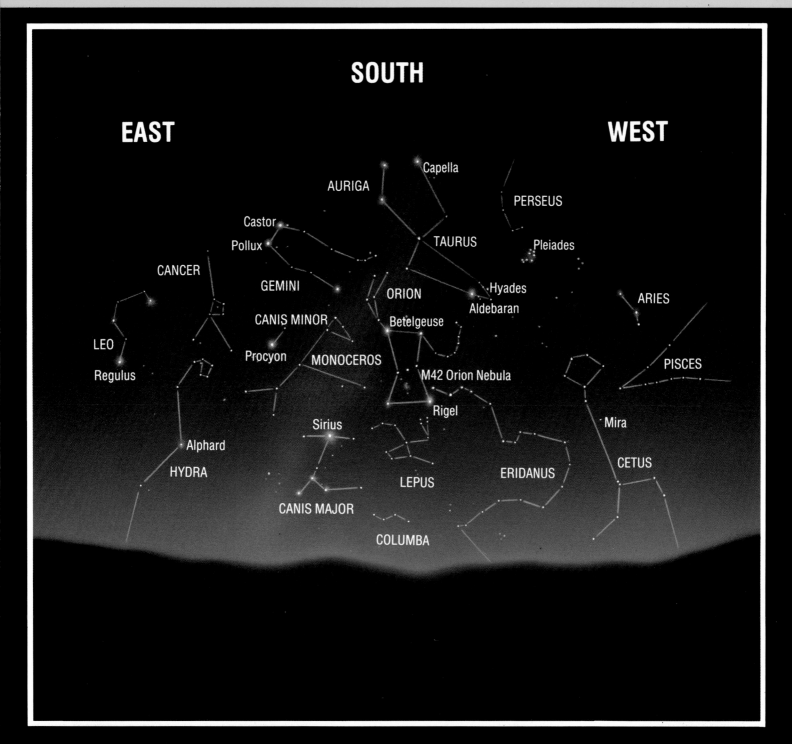

SOUTH

EAST

WEST

Capella

AURIGA

PERSEUS

Castor

Pollux

TAURUS

Pleiades

CANCER

GEMINI

ORION

Hyades

ARIES

Aldebaran

CANIS MINOR

Betelgeuse

LEO

Procyon

MONOCEROS

M42 Orion Nebula

PISCES

Regulus

Rigel

Mira

Sirius

Alphard

CETUS

HYDRA

LEPUS

ERIDANUS

CANIS MAJOR

COLUMBA

be found in the northeastern sky with Cassiopeia dropping towards the northwest.

The Milky Way is also well placed during the winter, passing from Cassiopeia in the northwest, through the overhead point and along through Auriga, to the west of Gemini, and the east of Orion and Canis Major. As was the case in summer, the Milky Way abounds in rich star fields and rewards time spent observing it with binoculars or a small telescope.

WINTER STARS
looking south

GLOSSARY

ASTEROID	Another name for a MINOR PLANET.
BINARY STAR	A pair of STARS which orbit each other in space.
BLACK HOLE	A region of space around a very massive STAR which has collapsed into a superdense body. Not even light can escape from a black hole.
CHROMOSPHERE	The part of the SUN's atmosphere which lies above the PHOTOSPHERE.
COMET	An object made up of gas, dust and ice which travels around the SUN in an ORBIT that is usually long and narrow.
CORONA	The outermost part of the SUN's atmosphere.
DOUBLE STAR	A STAR with two components. The STARS in a double star can be genuinely associated with each other (see BINARY STAR) or can only appear to lie close to each other because they lie in nearly the same direction as seen from EARTH.
EARTH	The third PLANET out from the SUN.
ECLIPSE	The covering up of one celestial object (such as the SUN) by another (such as the MOON).
FACULAE	Very bright patches of gas seen just above the areas on the SUN where SUNSPOTS are about to form.
GALAXY	Huge collections of STARS, gas, dust and other objects.
GAS GIANT PLANETS	The four largest planets Jupiter, Saturn, Uranus and Neptune which are comprised mainly of gas.
JUPITER	The largest PLANET and the fifth PLANET out from the SUN.
LIGHT YEAR	A unit of distance used by astronomers express distances in space. A light year is the distance light, moving at just over 186,000 miles per second, travels in a year. This is almost six trillion miles. (A trillion is taken to be a million million).
LOCAL GROUP	The group of GALAXIES of which our own GALAXY is a member.
MARS	The fourth PLANET out from the SUN.
METEOR	A streak of light seen darting across the sky, which is caused by the destruction of a METEOROID through friction with atmospheric particles.
METEORITE	A METEOROID which is large enough to at least partially survive the passage through the EARTH's atmosphere.
METEOROID	A particle of interplanetary debris.
MILKY WAY	The faint band of light seen crossing the sky which is the result of the combined light from thousands of STARS which lie in our GALAXY. Our GALAXY is often referred to as the Milky Way Galaxy.
MINOR PLANET	One of the many small objects which ORBIT the SUN between MARS and JUPITER. Also known as ASTEROIDS.
MOON	The EARTH'S only natural SATELLITE.

NEBULA	An interstellar cloud of gas and dust.
NEPTUNE	The eighth PLANET out from the SUN.
NEUTRON STAR	The very dense remnant of a STAR which has collapsed through the effects of gravity near the end of its life. Many neutron stars are formed after the original STAR has exploded as a SUPERNOVA.
NOVA	A STAR which suddenly, and unpredictably, flares in brightness before fading back to normal.
ORBIT	The path of one object (such as a PLANET) around another (such as the SUN)
PENUMBRA	The lighter part of a SUNSPOT surrounding the UMBRA. Also the name given to the area of partial shadow seen during an ECLIPSE.
PHOTOSPHERE	The bright, visible surface of the SUN.
PLANET	One of the nine major objects travelling around the SUN.
PLUTO	The smallest and outermost PLANET.
PROMINENCE	A mass of gas erupting from the surface of the SUN.
SATURN	The sixth PLANET out from the SUN.
STAR	A luminous object that produces light and heat through nuclear reactions at its core.
SOLAR SYSTEM	The system, dominated by the Sun, which includes the nine major planets, the minor planets, comets and all other objects that orbit the Sun.
SOLAR WIND	The stream of energized particles given off by the SUN.
SATELLITE	A smaller object (such as the MOON) in ORBIT around a larger one (such as the EARTH).
SUN	The STAR which is the dominant member of the SOLAR SYSTEM.
SUNSPOT	Dark areas seen on the PHOTOSPHERE of the SUN.
SUPERNOVA	The colossal explosion marking the end of a very massive STAR.
TERRESTERIAL PLANETS	The far inner, rocky planets Mercury, Venus, Earth and Mars. The word comes from an old word meaning "Earthlike".
UMBRA	The dark, central part of a SUNSPOT. Also the name given to the dark, central region of shadow seen during an ECLIPSE.
UNIVERSE BEYOND	Space beyond the Solar System.
URANUS	The seventh PLANET out from the SUN.
VARIABLE STAR	A STAR which is seen to vary in brightness, the variations being due either to changes taking place within the STAR itself or to the passage of one member of a BINARY STAR system in front of the other.
VENUS	The second PLANET out from the SUN.
WHITE DWARF	A small and very dense STAR which has used up most of its nuclear fuel and is at a very late stage in its life.